FUTURE FILES

COSMIC JOURNEYS

A BEGINNER'S GUIDE TO SPACE AND TIME TRAVEL

Written by
SARAH ANGLISS

COPPER BEECH BOOKS
BROOKFIELD, CONNECTICUT

© Aladdin Books Ltd 1998
© U.S. text 1998
Designed and produced by
Aladdin Books Ltd
28 Percy Street
London W1P 0LD

First published in the United States in 1998 by
Copper Beech Books,
an imprint of
The Millbrook Press
2 Old New Milford Road
Brookfield, Connecticut 06804

Editor
Simon Beecroft

Design
David West
Children's Book Design

Designer
Malcolm Smythe

Picture Research
Brooks Krikler Research

Illustrators
Stephen Sweet, Stuart Squires (Simon Girling
Associates), Mike Saunders, Ross Watton,
Alex Pang, Pat Murray

Printed in Belgium

Library of Congress Cataloging-in-Publication Data
Angliss, Sarah.
Cosmic journeys : a beginner's guide to space and time
travel / by Sarah Angliss ; illustrated by Alex Pang,
Mike Saunders, and Ross Watton.
p. cm. — (Future files)
Includes index.
Summary: Looks at the future of space travel including
nuclear fission-powered spacecraft, teleporting,
and time travel.
ISBN 0-7613-0635-8 (pbk.). —
ISBN 0-7613-0620-X (lib. bdg.).
1. Space and time—Juvenile literature. 2. Space flight—
Juvenile literature. 3. Outer space—Juvenile literature.
[1.Space and time. 2. Space flight. 3. Outer space.]
I. Pang, Alex, ill. II. Saunders, Mike, ill.
III. Watton, Ross, ill. IV. Title. V. Series.
QC173.59.S65A54 1998   97-41601
629.4'1—dc21   CIP AC
5 4 3 2 1

CONTENTS

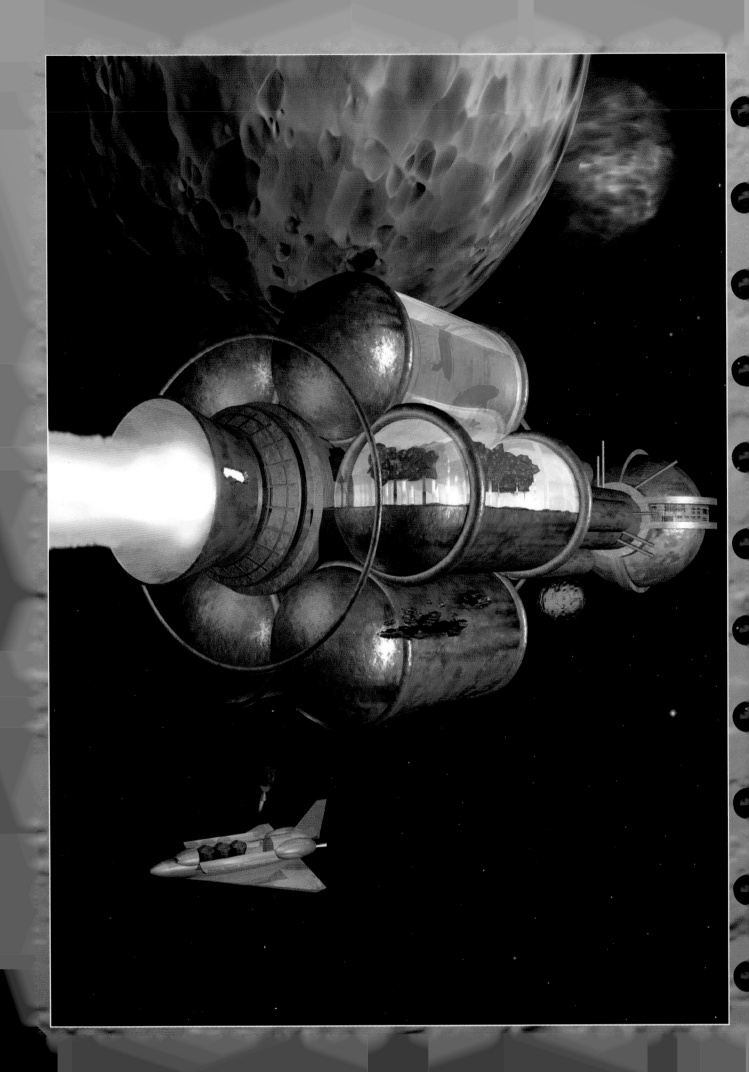

INTO THE FUTURE

EVER SINCE the first humans migrated around the world about one million years ago, we have never lost our passion for exploration. Now we are living in a very exciting era. For the first time in Earth's history, its inhabitants are able to leave the planet and embark on a voyage into the universe.

Although we are only just beginning this cosmic journey, we have already learned much about living beyond Earth.

Research on the space station *Mir* has helped us find ways to survive in space for many months. One day, we may be ready to embark on a long journey to another planet — or even to a distant star. To do this, we will need to invent faster or more sophisticated types of spaceships.

As our technology flourishes, we are learning more about the universe. New imaging devices allow us to look deeper into space than ever before.

These devices include the *Hubble Space Telescope* (*see* page 18) and satellites like *COBE* (*Cosmic Background Explorer*, *see* page 20).

Meanwhile, advances in physics are forcing us to look at space and time in completely new ways. We are now considering the notion that we might live in one of many parallel universes (*see* pages 28-29).

Incredible as it may sound, the journey into space may only be the first step into the unknown. One day we may want to look for a door from this universe into the next...

Right *Need to tell science fact from science fiction? Take a look at our Reality Check boxes. We can't see into the future, but these cunning devices tell you how realistic an idea is. The more green lights, the better. The "how soon?" line guesses when in the future the idea could be made: each green light is 50 years (so in the example here, it's 100 years in the future).*

REALITY CHECK

FEASIBLE TECHNOLOGY	○	●	●	●	●
SCIENCE IS SOUND	○	●	●	●	●
AFFORDABLE	○	●	●	○	●
HOW SOON?	●	●	○	●	●

THE FINAL FRONTIER

"Have you come from outer space?" asked the farmworkers. "Yes!" came the reply.

When Yuri Gagarin landed in a remote field in Asia on April 12, 1961, he had fulfilled a dream that was as old as humankind. Although the official welcoming party wasn't there to greet him, the Russian cosmonaut Gagarin had been the first person to journey successfully into space.

SPACE RACE

Orbiting the Earth in *Vostok 1*, Gagarin's mission focused the Earth's attention on the possibility of exploring other worlds. Before the decade was over, NASA had put astronauts on the Moon. On July 20, 1969, a billion people watched in awe as men from the *Apollo 11* mission took their first tentative steps outside the Earth. Science fiction had at last become science fact.

Below *A two-seater lunar rover was folded and packed into one small cabinet on its trip to the Moon in the later Apollo missions.*

Left *Featuring aliens that live under the Moon's crust, Jules Verne's fantasy* From the Earth to the Moon *was written over 100 years before the real Moon landings.*

NO CHEAP THRILL

According to some estimates, an *Apollo* mission to the Moon today would cost a staggering $500 billion to fund. Scientists need to find cheaper ways to explore space. They have already sent robot probes to our solar system and beyond. These have brought back spellbinding images of our neighboring worlds. The farthest reaching probe, *Pioneer 10*, is now over 6 billion miles (10 billion kilometers) from Earth. That's roughly 100 times the distance from the Earth to the Sun. In October 1997, NASA launched a new probe, *Cassini*, that will take a closer look at the rings and moons of Saturn.

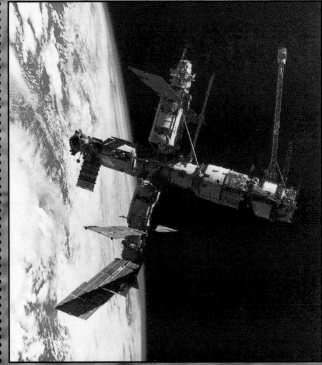

Right *Scientists on the space station* Mir *have studied how to support life for several months in space. This has help them plan future missions.*

BACK TO THE MOON

Under its dusty surface, the Moon may be rich in valuable minerals. The Apollo astronauts only brought back 840lb (382kg) of Moon rock, but some scientists think that we should go back and mine the Moon.

REACH FOR THE STARS

Scientists have not only set their sights on exploring the solar system — the nine planets, including Earth, that orbit our star, the Sun. One day they hope to reach other stars that lie far beyond. Interstellar travel is no mean feat. The nearest star, *Proxima Centauri*, is a staggering 25 million million miles away. Light, the fastest thing in the universe, takes over four years to travel that far, so scientists say this star is over four "light years" away.

FUEL PARADOX

If scientists want a crew to reach another star within a single lifetime, they will need to make a very fast spacecraft. This means they will have to build an engine that can rapidly accelerate it (speed it up). Spacecraft can be accelerated by rockets. The faster a rocket burns fuel, the more it will accelerate. Unfortunately though, a rocket that burns fuel quickly will need to carry lots of fuel to get to its destination. This will make it very heavy, so it will be hard to accelerate out of Earth's atmosphere.

BUILT FOR SPEED

Scientists designing tomorrow's rockets have taken their inspiration from the stars themselves. Ordinary rockets burn fuels like liquid hydrogen to make heat — but stars make heat in a process called nuclear fusion (see box, *above*). This releases huge amounts of energy from even the smallest quantity of fuel.

NUCLEAR FUSION

Nuclear fusion occurs when certain kinds of atoms are squeezed together at extremely high temperatures. The atoms fuse (join), releasing a huge burst of energy (and a few stray particles). Unfortunately, scientists think they will need more energy to run a fusion reactor than they will get out of it.

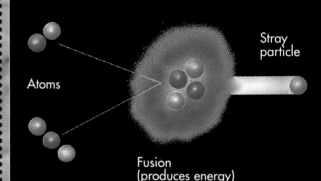

Atoms

Stray particle

Fusion (produces energy)

Left *Taking a year to travel to Mars, Viking 1 was powered by a small nuclear generator. The Viking Lander, carried by this craft, sent back the first-ever images of rocks on the Martian surface.*

NUCLEAR STARSHIP

FEASIBLE TECHNOLOGY	●●●●●
SCIENCE IS SOUND	●●●●●
AFFORDABLE	●●●●●
HOW SOON?	●●●●●

ON THE DRAWING BOARD

Designed for interstellar travel, this theoretical spaceship, Daedalus, would have a top speed of 60 million miles (100 million km) per hour, a tenth of the speed of light. Driven by 250 nuclear explosions per second, Daedalus would take four years to reach this speed. Although it has no room for passengers, it could travel to Barnard's Star, six light years away, and send information back to Earth within 50 years.

NUCLEAR FISSION

Some materials, such as one form of the metal uranium, are unstable — they break down, releasing energy and forming other materials. This is nuclear fission. At the heart of a nuclear power station, particles are fired at materials like this to release energy.

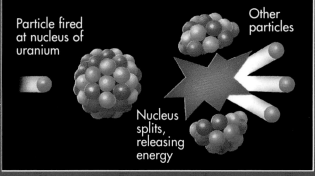

Particle fired at nucleus of uranium

Other particles

Nucleus splits, releasing energy

FULL SPEED AHEAD!

In programs like *Star Trek*, spaceships travel more swiftly than light, the fastest thing in the universe. In fact, the fastest spaceships we have built reach speeds that are less than one thousandth of the speed of light. But space scientists are looking for ways to improve on this.

POWER FROM ANTIMATTER

Science-fiction writers have suggested we could propel a craft with a matter-antimatter drive. Matter is the substance of which all things are made. Antimatter also exists in the universe, but is made only in extraordinary circumstances, such as when stars collide. It is opposite to matter in its electrical charge and many other characteristics. When matter and antimatter meet, they destroy each other, disappearing in a huge burst of energy. Scientists know that a reactor that brought matter and antimatter together would be a powerful energy source. Unfortunately, building such a reactor would be far from easy. As antimatter is so rarely found in the universe, scientists can only make it in expensive, energy-consuming experiments.
Even if they could make lots of antimatter, they would find it very hard to store. This is because it blows up any material it touches.

Above *Minute quantities of antimatter are made for fleeting moments in machines called particle accelerators, like this one in Geneva, Switzerland. The reaction is so expensive to produce, though, that one milligram of antimatter would cost more than 350 billion dollars!*

Left *If scientists could make one, a matter-antimatter spaceship could reach the Moon in an hour, Mars in a week, and Pluto, usually the most distant planet in our solar system, in a month.*

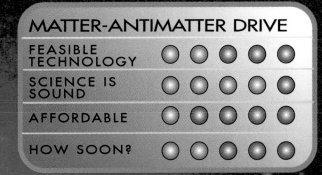

MATTER-ANTIMATTER DRIVE

FEASIBLE TECHNOLOGY	●	●	●	●	●
SCIENCE IS SOUND	●	●	●	●	●
AFFORDABLE	●	●	●	●	●
HOW SOON?	●	●	●	●	●

COSMIC FUNNEL

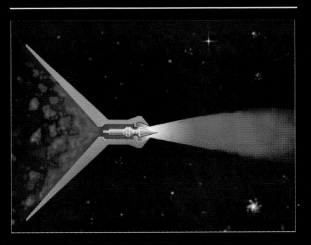

Scooping up hydrogen in space, this interstellar ramjet *would be a very fast spaceship. Its giant funnel would squeeze the hydrogen atoms into a nuclear fusion reactor, in order to generate continuous nuclear power.*

WARP FACTOR

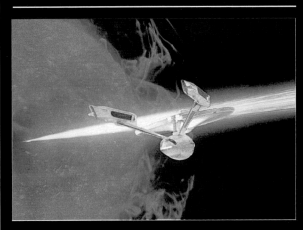

In Star Trek, the USS Enterprise uses matter-antimatter reactions to power its engine. In the original series, Chief Engineer Scotty is always fussing over his "dilithium crystals" — rods that control the speed of the matter-antimatter reactions.

LIGHT FANTASTIC

On a long journey to another star, we may not find a place to refuel. And if we wanted our spacecraft to carry enough fuel for the whole trip, it would be too vast to build. Before we can enjoy the prospect of interstellar travel, we will have to design a craft that works without an onboard energy supply. Here are just a few ideas that scientists are experimenting with on paper.

THE BIG PUSH

Space scientists think they could use high-powered laser or microwave beams to push spacecraft along. The U.S. military has already researched how high-powered lasers perform in space. Perhaps one day their knowledge could be used for a more peaceful project: reaching the stars.

Above *As part of their now-scaled-down defense program, code-named* Star Wars, *the U.S. military proposed using laser beams to shoot down missiles in space.*

BEAM US UP

Many science-fiction fans hope that we will one day use machines called transporters to travel from place to place. These will move us by turning us into beams of energy. Computers will store the information necessary to reassemble us at our destination. However, no one has yet come up with a way to turn us into pure energy. Even if they could, it is unlikely we could ever build a computer powerful enough to store all the data needed to remake a person.

LIGHT WORK

Powered by the Sun, this satellite could produce a narrow beam of microwave energy (just like the energy that cooks food in a microwave oven). Its energy beam could be pointed at a lightweight probe to propel the probe through space. To date, microwave propulsion systems only exist on paper.

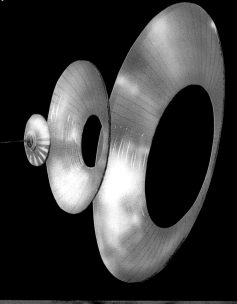

Above *A popular feature of* Star Trek, *the transporter was originally devised to cut the cost of making the program. It let characters visit planets without having to land a spaceship.*

A "lightsail" is a starship that would sail through space like a yacht. But instead of wind, its enormous, rigid metal disk would be pushed along by photons — individual particles that make up light. The craft would slowly continue to accelerate for years, eventually reaching incredibly high speeds. It could travel vast distances without any fuel on board.

HUGE MESH

Scientists have designed a probe called a "starwisp" that would be driven by a beam of microwaves. With a giant wire mesh sail, it would be 0.6 mile (1 km) in diameter but no heavier than a few sheets of paper. In theory, it could reach Proxima Centauri, the nearest star to our Sun, in less than 20 years.

SPACE ARKS · Mobile homes for generations of travelers

Earth has been our home for five million years. But we cannot assume we will be able to live here forever. If the climate changed dramatically, or a huge asteroid headed our way, or the Sun itself began to die, we would have to be ready to pack up our bags.

THE BIG SLEEP

If survivors from planet Earth were to go in search of another home on a faraway planet, they may find themselves traveling for decades, even centuries, through space. Some people have proposed that a huge starship called a space ark could be built to provide artificial worlds for generations of travelers. The interstellar voyagers may also wish to extend their lives in some way — or shorten their experience of the journey. Just as animals hibernate for the winter, it may be possible to put humans into an extended form of hibernation called hypersleep.

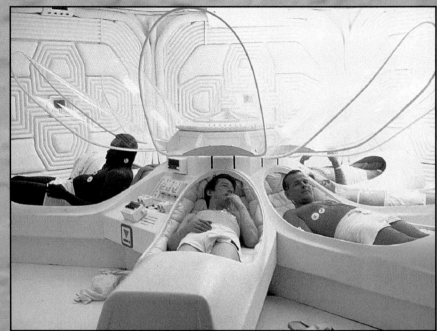

Above *The spine-chilling movie* Alien *(1979) starts with a strange life force waking the crew of the* Nostromo *from their hypersleep.*

DEEP FREEZE

Scientists involved in the controversial *Project Proteus* aim to develop hypersleep technology within 20 years. Their first step is to find out how to freeze nerve and brain cells without damaging them. Many scientists, however, doubt that hypersleep would slow down aging.

UNDER COVER

One giant asteroid could destroy our Earth by colliding with it, but another could become a refuge for a band of survivors. A space ark inside a hollowed-out asteroid would be protected against impacts with other objects.

Rotation provides artificial gravity

A green world could be created inside the asteroid

A space ark would need foolproof sensors to monitor humans in hypersleep and to wake them up at the right time. Computer-controlled systems would regulate the temperature and pressure around the preserved survivors.

ARK WORLD

There is roughly 1,300 sq miles (3,500 sq km) of living area inside this space ark. Proposed by NASA scientists, it has several habitats, including countryside, lakes, forests, and towns. This would be the only world that generations would know.

SPACE ARK

FEASIBLE TECHNOLOGY	●	●	●	●	●
SCIENCE IS SOUND	●	●	●	●	●
AFFORDABLE	●	●	●	●	●
HOW SOON?	●	●	●	●	●

SPACE WARS · The battle for cosmic supremacy

When American astronauts hoisted the U.S. flag on the Moon in 1969, they were continuing a tradition that is as old as history. Humans are territorial creatures — when they find new land, they want to claim it for themselves. Flag-raising on the Moon was just a gesture. But as we strip Earth of its fuels and minerals, people may start fighting in earnest over new worlds in space.

Left In Independence Day (1996), *aliens attempted to destroy life on Earth.*
Below The AT-ATs *in* The Empire Strikes Back *(1980) weren't too friendly either. Let's hope real aliens would be more civilized than these fantasy creatures.*

MOSTLY FRIENDLY?

Excitement about possible life on Mars shows our longing to know we are not alone. Contact with alien life is the dream of many scientists — but it's often a nightmare in science fiction. While scientists hope we'll exchange knowledge with alien civilizations, science-fiction writers think we will be exchanging blows.

SURVIVAL

Whether we are fighting among ourselves or against an alien civilization, war is an expression of our most basic instinct. The goal of war is to prove to your opponent that you are the more likely to survive. Hopefully, as we reach out farther into space, we will be able to override these instincts and share the universe in peace.

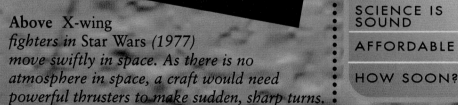

Above X-wing *fighters in* Star Wars (1977) *move swiftly in space. As there is no atmosphere in space, a craft would need powerful thrusters to make sudden, sharp turns.*

WAR IN SPACE

FEASIBLE TECHNOLOGY	●	●	●	●	●
SCIENCE IS SOUND	●	●	●	●	●
AFFORDABLE	●	●	●	●	●
HOW SOON?	○	○	○	○	○

NO DRAG

There's no need for this Destroyer to be streamlined, as there's no air in space for it to cut through. Clunky, box-shaped spaceships would have no trouble traveling swiftly through space.

DEADLY HARDWARE?

In science fiction, force fields can make enemy missiles bounce off a spaceship and traction beams can pull up an enemy craft. But that's science fiction — no one has really built such ingenious devices.

INTO THE UNKNOWN

Look up at a clear night sky and you'll see that space is full of stars. We already know that some stars, like the anonymous-sounding *PSR B1257 + 12*, have planets, just like our own star, the Sun. Rather than waiting for aliens to drop in on Earth, scientists are now looking for distant worlds that extraterrestrials might live on. Ultimately, they hope to find a rare jewel: a planet just like Earth that we could make a second home.

FAINT HOPE

Viewed from just a few light years away, a planet similar to Earth would be so faint, it would be swamped by light from its star. That is why astronomers can only seek out planets indirectly — by spotting telltale signs that they are in orbit.

Right *In 1994, a huge comet called Shoemaker-Levy 9 smashed into the planet Jupiter, exploding with the force of trillions of megatons of high explosives. Earth is fortunate to be shielded from such collisions by the other planets around it. Would other habitable planets be as fortunate as Earth?*

Above *Looking further into the universe than any other optical telescope, the* Hubble Space Telescope *may help us to find another Earth.*

Above *In the sci-fi comedy* Men in Black *(1997), thousands of aliens have already made Earth their home. Human agents working undercover zap the memory of anyone who notices this alien presence.*

PULL OF A PLANET

As planets cannot be seen around a star, scientists have to find clever ways to detect them. Scientists know that planets have an effect on nearby stars: They make them wobble. They also know that planets make the light from a star flicker slightly when the planets pass in front of it. Using a branch of space science called astrometry, scientists hope to measure changes in a star's behavior to determine if it has any planets in orbit.

CALLING LONG DISTANCE

If we find a new planet, we still need to know if anything lives on it, or even if it is habitable. It would have to be the right distance from its star, so it wouldn't be too hot or too cold.

If we found a habitable planet that was a great distance from Earth, a human colony living on it would have problems phoning their loved ones back at home. Radio waves would be used to send messages to and from Earth but radio waves do not travel any faster than light. So, for someone on a new Earthlike planet three light years away, it would take three years to send a message home. The person would also need to wait three more years to hear a reply.

IS THERE ANYTHING OUT THERE?

The European Space Agency (ESA) has proposed a system that could scan distant planets for signs of a breathable atmosphere. Pairs of telescopes on Earth and in space, are linked up to form, in effect, one huge telescope, with an enormous range. By picking up infra-red radiation (energy given off by things that are hot), this telescope system would be able to study the atmospheres of planets many light years away.

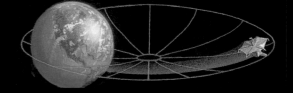

SPACE-TIME · The fourth dimension and the shape of the universe

We think of ourselves as three-dimensional beings: We have a height, a width, and a breadth. With space technology, we may have the potential to travel millions of miles through the three dimensions of space. But we are also on a continual journey through a fourth dimension: time.

THE SHAPE OF SPACE

Scientists use the term "space-time" to describe the four dimensions of the universe. The work of the scientist Albert Einstein is very important to our understanding of space-time. According to Einstein, any object with mass — from a speck of dust to a star — curves the space and time around it. This creates gravity. This has led many people to wonder about the overall shape of the universe. Is it curved? If we traveled along one of its dimensions would we end up where we started? Has its shape changed over time?

Above *Although a genius, Albert Einstein made one big mistake. He assumed the Universe has always been the same size.*

EXPANDING UNIVERSE

Most scientists agree that the universe is expanding. This expansion is thought to have started with the Big Bang about 15 billion years ago, when the universe exploded into being. Everything in the universe now constantly moves away from everything else. The farther away a star is, the faster it speeds away from Earth.

But stars and other objects in the universe are not simply separating from each other in the way that balls move apart on a billiard table. The space and time they occupy is expanding as well — as though the billiard table itself were growing.

Some scientists are now wondering if time only moves forward because of this expansion. No one knows whether the universe will continue expanding forever. Some people think that if it started to shrink again, time would reverse and go backward.

Above *The COBE (Cosmic Background Explorer) satellite has picked up the extremely faint echoes of the Big Bang, the huge explosion thought to have created the universe.*

Right *This bright galaxy, called a quasar, is over 3 billion light years away. Quasars are thought to be the most distant objects in the universe.*

NEW DIMENSIONS

Captured by the Hubble Space Telescope, *light from this distant nebula (dust cloud) has taken 12 billion years to reach us. So we are seeing the nebula as it looked 12 billion years ago — only 3 billion years after the Big Bang! Our universe has four dimensions, but there could be other universes that have more (or fewer). The laws of physics would still work in hyperspace — a place that has many dimensions.*

HYPERSPACE

FEASIBLE TECHNOLOGY	● ● ● ● ●
SCIENCE IS SOUND	● ● ● ● ●
AFFORDABLE	● ● ● ● ●
HOW SOON?	● ● ● ● ●

TIME TRAVEL · Paradoxes, problems, and parallel universes

Time travel is one of the most exciting ideas in science fiction. By stepping into a time machine, a person is able to set the controls for any date (past or future) and the machine takes them there in an instant. The person in the time machine would be the same age they were when they got in. Most scientists think that time travel will never be possible. The space-time expert, Stephen Hawking, for example, believes it is unlikely that a time machine will be invented in the future: Otherwise we would already have been visited by time travelers.

PAST MASTERS

The movie *Back to the Future* (1985) shows us one of the biggest problems with the idea of time travel. When the hero Marty McFly goes back 30 years, he violates something that physicists call "causality" (one thing leads to another). He meets his mother and father when they are teenagers, and stops them from falling in love. This, in turn, means that he is never born — so he can never travel back in time to meet them in the first place. Disrupting causality can be a very confusing business.

SAME OLD STORY

Some scientists, including the philosopher David Deutsch, think that Marty could have traveled back in time quite safely. They argue that anyone who goes back to the past would be forced, by the laws of physics, not to alter history. Even if Marty wanted to stop his parents from falling in love, he would be prevented from doing so. If he decided to shoot his father for instance, something would stop him from pulling the trigger. The laws of physics will make sure what must happen, does happen.

Alternatively, some scientists argue that Marty *can* change the course of history, but only in a "parallel" universe — that is, he would have created a new universe that exists alongside the other one. He and his family still exist, as they always have done, in the universe that he came from.

FAMILY MATTERS

With help from a local scientist, Marty is able to change his parents' lives as teenagers so they end up happy and successful when he goes back to his own time. Many scientists think his revamped family would live with him in a parallel universe. He'd still be with the same old unhappy family in the universe he originally came from.

Above *The science-fiction movie* Millennium *(1989) shows a chilling use of time travel. When, 1,000 years in the future, humans are dying out, they go back to the past to steal bodies, which are used to keep the human race going.*

TIME MACHINE

FEASIBLE TECHNOLOGY	○ ○ ○ ○ ○
SCIENCE IS SOUND	○ ○ ○ ○ ○
AFFORDABLE	○ ○ ○ ○ ○
HOW SOON?	○ ○ ○ ○ ○

BLACK HOLES · Doors to other universes or deadly dead ends?

Above *Cosmic researcher, Stephen Hawking, thinks the universe is peppered with black holes of all sizes, large and small.*

When we launch a rocket into space, we need to make it move fast enough to escape the pull of the Earth's gravity. If Earth were heavier or denser (more tightly packed), our rocket would need to go faster. Now imagine an object that is so heavy and dense that not even light — the fastest thing in the universe — can travel quickly enough to escape it. An object like this is called a black hole.

DEAD STARS

Black holes aren't just science fiction — scientists think they really do exist. They could be formed when massive stars die, for example. Dying stars collapse in on themselves to leave super-heavy, super-dense remains. The remains could become so tightly packed, they form a black hole.

TOMORROW IS YESTERDAY

Some theorists have imagined how black holes could work like time machines. The gravity around a black hole could be so great that it would cause time and space to fold back on itself, creating a loop. If you traveled into this loop, you could find that time doesn't go forward as usual, but doubles back on itself. So you'd end up going back in time!

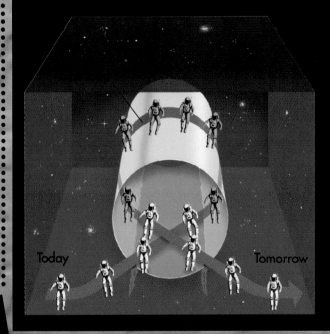

Today   Tomorrow

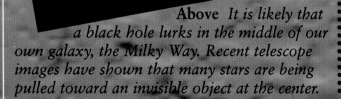

Above *It is likely that a black hole lurks in the middle of our own galaxy, the Milky Way. Recent telescope images have shown that many stars are being pulled toward an invisible object at the center.*

IN THE DARK

We will never be able to see a black hole as light cannot escape from it. But we can spot a black hole in action. As it creates a huge gravitational force, it pulls gas clouds and other stars toward it. Matter spiraling into a black hole heats up, giving off X rays that we can detect.

People have come up with lots of imaginative ideas about travel through black holes. Some suggest they could be gateways to other times or universes (see box *above*). But Stephen Hawking offers a word of caution. He doesn't think anyone could survive such journeys, even if they were possible.

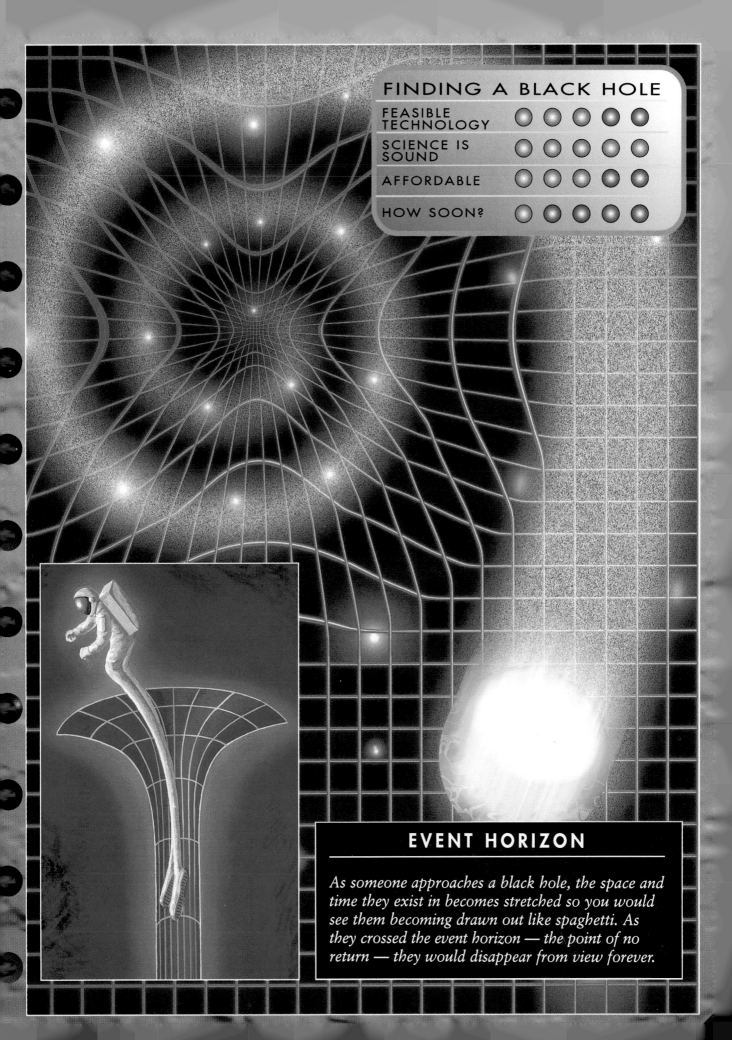

FINDING A BLACK HOLE

FEASIBLE TECHNOLOGY	○ ○ ○ ○ ○
SCIENCE IS SOUND	○ ○ ○ ○ ○
AFFORDABLE	○ ○ ○ ○ ○
HOW SOON?	○ ○ ○ ○ ○

EVENT HORIZON

As someone approaches a black hole, the space and time they exist in becomes stretched so you would see them becoming drawn out like spaghetti. As they crossed the event horizon — the point of no return — they would disappear from view forever.

WORMHOLES·

Shortcuts through space and time?

Need to get to the other side of the universe in no time at all? You should take a wormhole. Favored by science-fiction writers as the quickest way to travel to a whole new time or space, a wormhole is a tunnellike black hole that forms a shortcut from one part of the universe to another. If you would like to find a wormhole, you are not alone. So far, scientists have only studied wormholes on paper. Until they locate one in space, no one can be certain they exist.

WORMHOLES					
FEASIBLE TECHNOLOGY	●	●	●	●	●
SCIENCE IS SOUND	●	●	●	●	●
AFFORDABLE	○	●	●	●	●
HOW SOON?	●	●	●	●	●

A NEW TIME OR PLACE

If scientists find a way to travel through wormholes, they may be able to use them to travel through time as well as space. The scientist, Albert Einstein, and his colleague, Nathan Rosen, also imagined that these could be gateways to other universes. Ultimately, wormholes could be used to travel to other dimensions — if they exist (*see* page 28-29)

Below *In his novel* Contact *(made into a movie in 1997), physicist Carl Sagan wrote about a ship that safely journeyed through a wormhole. His ideas inspired a colleague, Kip Thorne, to imagine a way to stop wormholes from collapsing (see* right*).*

Above *In the movie* Time Bandits (1981), *a band of explorers takes shortcuts through space and time using a map of the universe that shows the locations of wormholes.*

SHORTCUT

From their calculations, physicists have already found that travel through a wormhole would be highly problematic. A wormhole would generate such a large force of gravity, it would collapse in on itself as soon as it appeared. So if you were lucky enough to spot an open wormhole, you would need to travel at a speed faster than light to get through it before the wormhole collapsed.

LOCKED OUT

Spacecraft can travel effortlessly through worm holes in science-fiction shows like Dr. Who *and* Deep Space Nine. *But physicists know using wormholes wouldn't really be that easy. Before we could travel through one, we would need to stop it from collapsing when it formed. Physicist Kip Thorne and his colleagues think we could keep a wormhole open using pressure. If applied in the right way, pressure could overcome the wormhole's gravitational forces by creating "antigravity." But even if we found a wormhole, and we could keep it open — would we survive the trip?*

WHEN REALITIES MEET

For some time, scientists have been considering the possibility that our universe is not the only one that exists. Many theorists believe there could be a vast number of universes, floating like bubbles in space. Science-fiction writers already play with this idea. Their characters often visit "parallel" universes, including some where time runs backward and others that have more dimensions than our own. These ideas should be viewed as more than pure fantasy. Amazingly, there is already some evidence that parallel universes exist — it's an experiment that can be tried in a laboratory.

DOUBLE TROUBLE

In the experiment, a photon (a single particle of light) is fired at a screen that has two narrow slits (*see* right). What happens next is astonishing. The photon doesn't go through just one of the two slits. It passes through both slits at once! Some scientists think that the photon goes through one slit in one universe (ours) and through the other slit in a parallel universe — one that exists so close to ours that it can interfere (cross over) with our own.

LIGHT FANTASTIC

When we see a single photon of light travel through two slits at once, we could be witnessing the crossover between events in two parallel universes.

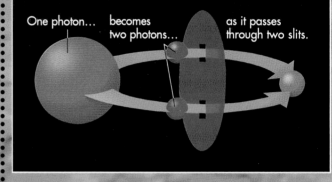

One photon... becomes two photons... as it passes through two slits.

TOWARD THE UNKNOWN

The possibility of parallel universes has stretched the imaginations of scientists and science-fiction writers to the limit. One thing is certain: Traveling beyond our own space and time to a new, parallel universe would be the ultimate cosmic journey.

Above Some people have fancifully suggested that ghosts are signs of "interference" between our universe and a parallel one.

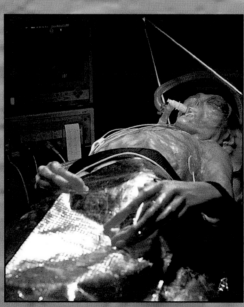

Above If aliens exist, they could live in other universes that have more dimensions than our own. They may not be able to exist in our space-time.

Above If UFOs are made by extraterrestrials, they may come from different universes — not just other worlds.

THE MULTIVERSE

According to one theory, whenever an event occurs, even something as simple as a particle moving through a slit or a person leaving through a door, another universe is formed. We are living in a giant "multiverse" that is teaming with universes, billions of which look very much like our own.

GLOSSARY

ACCELERATE
To increase in speed. The quicker something gains speed, the more it is accelerating.

ANTIGRAVITY
Something that creates forces between objects with mass, forcing them apart. In theory, antigravity can be used to counteract gravity.

ANTIMATTER
Curious stuff that has opposite characteristics to matter. Scientists have been able to make small amounts of antimatter in the laboratory.

ASTEROID
A lump of rock, usually less than a mile in diameter, that orbits the Sun. Most asteroids lie in a belt between Mars and Jupiter.

BIG BANG
The explosive event that may have created our universe about 15 billion years ago.

BLACK HOLE
An object that is so heavy and dense, not even light can escape it. Huge, dying stars may form black holes when they collapse in on themselves.

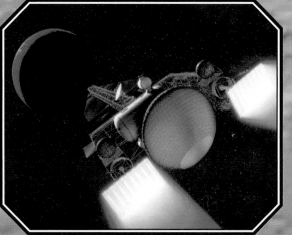

CAUSALITY
The basic principle that nothing can happen without a cause. For instance, you could not be reading this unless you had been born.

DENSE
Something tightly packed. Dense objects have a large mass but are relatively small in size.

DIMENSION
Something we can measure and move through. We live in three dimensions of space and one dimension of time.

ESA
The European Space Agency. ESA is responsible for designing and launching space probes used by European scientists.

EVENT HORIZON
The point of no return from a black hole. Nothing that crosses the event horizon would be able to escape the black hole's enormous force of gravity.

EXTRATERRESTRIALS
Living beings that do not come from Earth. So far, no firm evidence for the existence of extraterrestrials has been found.

GRAVITY
The phenomenon that creates a force between objects with mass, pulling them together. Heavy objects create a bigger force of gravity than light ones.

HYPERSLEEP
A deep form of hibernation that could possibly one day be used to preserve people traveling many light years through space.

HYPERSPACE
Space-time that contains far more dimensions than our own. Some other universes — if they exist — may have hyperspace.

INFRA-RED RADIATION
Waves of energy given off by objects that are hot. Infra-red radiation travels as fast as light.

INTERSTELLAR
Between the stars. Interstellar spacecraft are designed to survive the long journeys from one star to another.

LIGHT YEAR
The distance light can travel through empty space in one year. Roughly equal to 5.6 million million miles, a light year is useful for describing the vast distances between objects in space.

MASS
The amount of matter in an object.

MATTER
The stuff that anything with mass is made of. The heavier something is, the more matter it contains.

MATTER-ANTIMATTER REACTION
The reaction that takes place when matter and antimatter meet. The two substances obliterate each other, turning into pure energy.

MICROWAVE
A wave of energy that moves as fast as light. Microwaves are similar to radio waves but are easier to beam at narrow targets.

MILKY WAY
The galaxy that we live in, containing hundreds of billions of stars. The Milky Way is a disk-shaped galaxy that is over 80,000 light years in diameter.

MULTIVERSE
The place where many scientists think we live. The multiverse is made up of a huge number of parallel universes and is growing all the time.

NASA
The U.S. National Aeronautics and Space Administration. This is the organization that put the first people on the Moon.

NUCLEAR FISSION
The process by which heavy atoms, such as uranium, divide to make lighter ones, releasing energy.

NUCLEAR FUSION
The process by which light elements combine, or fuse, releasing energy and stray particles.

PARADOX
Two true statements that conflict with each other. Some scientists think we would create paradoxes if we traveled back in time. For example, if a time traveler were to go back in time and stop their parents from meeting, the time traveler would not be born. But then how could they have traveled back in time?

PARALLEL UNIVERSE
A universe that exists alongside — but separate from — our own. Some scientists think parallel universes are formed every time there is an event in history — even the smallest movement of a particle.

PHOTON
A single packet of light. A photon is the smallest amount of light that can exist.

SPACE-TIME
The four dimensions of space and time that we live in.

THEORETICAL
Describes an idea that *should* work, but has not yet been proved to work in practice.

WORMHOLE
A tunnellike black hole that acts as a shortcut to another place in the universe or even to another universe altogether.

INDEX